What is a Feast?

Josef Pieper, 1904-   *Photographer: Hilde Schurk-Frisch*

What is a Feast?
Josef Pieper

The Pascal Lectures on Christianity and the University
at the University of Waterloo, 1981

North Waterloo Academic Press
370 University Avenue East
Waterloo Ontario Canada N2K 2B5

B
56
.P53
1987

Copyright Josef Pieper 1987

All rights reserved. No part of this publication may be
reproduced or used in any form by any means – graphic,
electronic or mechanical, including photocopying,
recording, taping or information storage and retrieval
systems – without written permission of the North
Waterloo Acaemic Press.

International Standard Book Number 0-921-075-04-9

Canadian Cataloguing in Publication Data

Pieper, Josef, 1904-
    What is a feast?

(Pascal lectures on Christianity and the university)
"Pascal lectures on Christianity and the university at the University of
    Waterloo, 1981."
ISBN 0-921-075-04-9

1. Fasts and feasts.   2. Philosophy and religion.
3. Christianity – 20th century.   4. God.   I. Title.
II. Series.

B56,P53   1987   200'.1   C88-093028-4

North Waterloo Academic Press
370 University Avenue East
Waterloo, Ontario, Canada
N2K 2B5

Distributed in the United Kingdom by:
Grand Publications Ltd.
195 Banbury Road
Oxford, England OX2 7AR

Printed and bound in Canada by
John Deyell Company
Lindsay, Ontario 1987

Contents

Introduction *by John North* vii

What is a Feast? 1

Hope and History 25

**On the Unavoidable Dilemma of a
  Non-Christian Philosophy** 51

On Leisure 57

Index 67

Grateful acknowledgement is given to St. Jerome's College and the
University of Waterloo for support of this Lecture Series.

Other books by Josef Pieper

Leisure the Basis of Culture, 1952
The End of Time; a Meditation on the Philosophy of History, 1954
The Silence of St. Thomas; Three Essays, 1957
Fortitude and Temperance, 1954
Justice, 1957
Prudence, 1959
Scholasticism: Personalities and Problems of Medieval Philosophy, 1961
Introduction to Thomas Aquinas, 1962
Belief and Faith, 1963
Enthusiasm and Divine Madness; on the Platonic Dialogue of Phaedrus, 1964
The Four Cardinal Virtues, Prudence, Justice, Fortitude, Temperance, 1965
Reality and the Good, 1967
Death and Immortality, 1969
Hope and History, 1969
In Tune with the World; a Theory of Festivity, 1973
About Love, 1974
Guide to Thomas Aquinas, 1982
On Hope, 1986
No One Could Have Known: An Autobiography; the Early Years, 1987

Other Pascal Lecture Series publications available:

Malcolm Muggeridge, *The End of Christendom*, Eerdman's, 1978
Donald MacKay, *Science and the Quest for Meaning*, Eerdman's, 1979
Charles Malik, *A Christian Critique of the University*, North Waterloo
  Academic Press, Library Edition, 1988 (1981).

Introduction

> Man is obviously made for thinking. Therein lies all his dignity and his merit; and his whole duty is to think as he ought. Now the order of thought is to begin with ourselves, and with our author and our end.
>
> Blaise Pascal, *Pensée* 620

> Jesus Christ is the author of all things, the center to which all things tend. Whoever knows him knows the reason for all things.
>
> *Pensée* 450

This volume contains the four lectures delivered as the annual Pascal Lectures on Christianity and the University at the University of Waterloo, Ontario, Canada in November, 1981. Blaise Pascal (1623-62), the seventeenth-century French academic and Christian, is remembered today as a forerunner of Newton in his establishment of the calculus and as the author of his Christian meditations, *Les Pensées*. Members of the University of Waterloo, wishing to establish a forum for the presentation of Christian issues in an academic environment, have chosen to commemorate the life of Pascal by this annual event.

The Pascal Lectures bring to the University of Waterloo outstanding individuals of international repute who have distinguished themselves in both scholarly endeavor and Christian thought or life. These individuals discourse with the university community on some aspect of its own world, its theories, its research, its leadership role in our society, challenging the university to search for truth through personal faith and intellectual inquiry which focus on Jesus Christ.

Josef Pieper's philosophical books, fifty or more of them, have been translated into fourteen languages and have sold more than a million copies. Few if any other twentieth century philosphers speak with such power to so broad and receptive an audience. "Joseph of Arimathea" was the ringing greeting addressed to Pieper in church every Sunday throughout early boyhood by his special friend, the village blacksmith of Elte, Westphalia, Germany. The man had prophetic insight.

Pieper, born in 1904, too late by several years to fight in the first Great War, was tempered throughout the mental and spiritual growth of his young adulthood by encounters with the Nazi party. A Christian intellectual and Thomistic philosopher who resisted National Socialism, he found himself denied academic posts, so having to depend on his parents into his early thirties. His first book, on the Catholic Social Doctrine, which had been thrice reprinted, was banned in 1933 and had the remaining copies confiscated. His increasingly vocal resistance to the Third Reich made him vulnerable: not a pacifist, his military service was in an airforce unit (joined at the urging of like-minded friends) where his training in sociology and psychology suited him for a position assessing the leadership potential of pilots. Time after time in these years the events which loomed as disappointments, griefs, tragedies – even his time as a prisoner of war – proved to herald advantage and joy for him and his young family. But at the moment No One Could Have Known, as he implies in the title of Volume 1 of his autobiography.

After the war Pieper became a Professor at the University of Munster, where he still lectures as Professor Emeritus. For many years he has been in demand as visiting lecturer in Europe, the USA, Canada, Mexico, India and Japan. He has been awarded several honourary doctorates, the Aquinas Medal of the American Catholic Philosophical Association, and membership in the German Academy of Language and Poetry, the Academy of Sciences in Dusseldorf, and the Pontifical Academy of Thomas Aquinas in Rome. In 1987 he received the Richard M. Weaver Award for Scholarly Letters, and delivered his address "On Clarity" at the 1987 Ingersoll Prizes Awards Banquet.

****

The dismal Nazi 'celebrations' in December, 1943, prompted a response in Pieper which, some twenty years later, became a theory of festivity suggested by the title of this little volume, *What Is a Feast?* Can truly festive feasts be legislated now any more than by the Nazis, or for that matter, by the French Revolution two centuries ago? What are the essential elements of a festive occasion? Why are the amusements of the idle rich so desperately unfestive? In pursuing these questions he surveys the conclusions of a broad range of Western intellectuals: Rousseau, Nietzsche, Kurt Eisner, Karl Kerény, G.K. Chesterton, Julian and Aldous Huxley, Jean Paul Sartre, Soren Kierkegaard, August Comte, Josef Jungmann, Jacques Louis David, Trotzky, Gorki, Briand, Roger Caillois, Teilhard de Chardin, Bertolt Brecht. Then he reaches back through Western history to Plato, Aristotle, and the church fathers. His conclusion observes a contemporary "darkening of the world," movement toward a global war of annihilation, a delight in 'nausea', a revelling in 'absurdity' which actually desires to celebrate as an anti-festival so unspeakable a catastrophe. But the man who despairs has not yet received 'certain tidings,' tidings of the divine guarantee of the world and of human salvation.

He who dares to look at man, standing with the H-bomb in his hands and unmastered aggression in his heart, risks the loss of hope in the evolutionary process, Pieper says in his second essay, "Hope and History," referring to the well-known image given us by Konrad Lorenz. However dramatic the destructive power of modern technology, man has not changed since Cain; and the ultimate hope is for the self, not for the group. We all face death. Is there one hope, one "joyful expectation," one thing which will not come with the necessity of a law of nature, a single hope, the loss of which would make a man despair? When all other hopes fail, does one remain? Might this one even appear because all others fail? The object of such a hope is personal wholeness, self-realization in the future. Man's existence has the structure of 'not yet.' History, that which we make of what happens to us, may be said to be the field of hope. For what? Plato answers, for the common life of God and man on the other side of death, the banquet in which the soul participates, as a guest and companion of the gods, satisified by the contemplation of the highest being. Pieper considers the link between non-Christian and Christian on these issues, and the distinctiveness of Christianity.

The Unavoidable Dilemma of a Non-Christian Philosophy, he says in his third and shortest essay, is that while the great founders of Occidental philosophy (Pythagoras, Plato, Aristotle) see it to require an unprejudiced openness to theology, a loving aiming at the wisdom which God alone possesses, the secularized modern European or North American, who is the product of several hundred years of philosophical rationalism, does not know what 'wisdom in divine affairs' means, nor where it can be found. The left-liberals in philosophic thought (excluding that group which pursues linguistic analysis and scientific 'philosophy,' not claiming to be philosophers in any traditional sense), improbably will accept a non-obscure, non-ambiguous and adequate theology. Thus their dilemma.

Finally, in his essay on "Leisure," Professor Pieper begins with a definition of work as laborious activity with a useful social function. In contemporary life passiveness is thought to be senseless; work is overvalued; men are known as 'workers.' Utility demands to be the measure of all things, including 'spare time' and even the intellectual life of the university. This incapacity for leisure implies the incapacity for celebrating a feast. And a feast has always meant the affirmation of man's fundamental accord with God and with himself and with the world. So leisure opposes an excessive emphasis on social function; it releases man from his status as a 'worker.' Leisure frees man from both inhuman work and idleness. This view of the Christians is shared by Plato, who says that only in celebrating divine worship does man lose the shape of a slave, and by Aristotle, declaring that man can live a life of leisure only in so far as something divine dwells within him. Pieper is in fundamental agreement with Pascal, that Christianity's being not unique is far from being a reason for believing it not to be true. On the contrary, it is what proves it to be so *(Pensée 747).*

The succinctness with which Pieper sums up these four major themes of his life, expressing the relation of each to the other, is unique to this edition of his work. His life has virtually spanned the twentieth century, withstanding by grace and commenting on man's self-destructiveness within the century, providing a context reaching backwards thousands of years and testifying of a hope stretching into and beyond the future. Indeed, his life is a demonstration of solidarity with Blaise Pascal, who proclaims, "Truth is so obscured nowadays and lies are so well established that unless we love the truth we shall never recognize it."

John North
Department of English
University of Waterloo

What is a Feast?

What is a feast? At first sight the question seems to be quite easily answerable. Does not everyone know what a feast is–a festival, a festivity? Besides, the question seems to be not especially urgent. Let us consider first the point of answerability. It is rather likely that whoever tries to answer that question will have the same experience as St. Augustine did with regard to the question, not of festivity, but of time. "If no one asks me," he said, "I know; but if I wish to explain it to one who asks, I know not." The problem is to put into words what everyone means and knows.

And indeed, we are very forcefully 'asked,' both what a feast is, and, even more, what the human prerequisites are for celebrating a feast. After all, the failure of our festivals, the difficulty of celebrating a feastday festively, is well known to us all. "The trick is not to arrange a festival, but to find people who can enjoy it"–this is a quotation from the posthumous writings of Friedrich Nietzsche, who wrote it down almost one hundred years ago. The sentence implies no less than that festivity in general is in danger of extinction, for it is obvious that a festival does not come about by arrangements alone. But Nietzsche is not the only European thinker who comes to such a conclusion. In 1906 a brilliant and at the same time confused pamphlet was published under the title,

2 What is a Feast?

Feste der Festlosen (*Festivals of the Unfestive*). The title sums up the whole argument. The author was the Communist intellectual, Kurt Eisner. One of his statements is this: "Perhaps the time is approaching when festivals, as mass manifestations of an intensified sense of life, will be nothing more than curiosities to be studied from old pictures and artifacts preserved in ethnological museums." In the meantime it has become a more or less standard matter, and even a matter of literary fashion, to connect the "misery of this present age" with "man's incapacity for festivity."

For the time being, I suspect that this gloomy diagnosis oversimplifies a bit. The chances are it has never been easy in any age to meet the requirement that great festivals be celebrated in the proper spirit. As the history of religion tells us, empty and wearisome pomp existed even at the famous Greek festivals. Nevertheless it seems to be peculiar to our time that we may conceive of festivity itself as being expressly repudiated–which indeed would be something new and unheard of. It is this very situation which gives rise to the question which we are facing, and which prompts us to determine for ourselves what presumably everybody knows and takes for granted; namely, what the essence of festivity is, and what should be done so that men in our time may preserve or regain the capacity to celebrate real festivals festively–a capacity which concerns the heart of life and perhaps constitutes it. Once again, what is a feast? Mere description of classical or medieval or East Indian festivals, no matter how accurate and stirring, does not answer the question at all. It does not even touch the question. We must attack it in a far more fundamental sense.

Certain things can be adequately discussed only if we speak at the same time of the whole of the world and of life. If we are not ready to do that, we give up all claim to saying anything significant at all. Death and love are such subjects. But festivity, too, must be included in this category. This becomes apparent as soon as we try to get beyond mere description of the facts.

If, for instance, we start with what lies nearest at hand, and consider the distinction between the festive and the workaday, we soon realize that the antithesis belongs to quite a different category from, say, that of left and right, or day and night. We do not mean only that a working day and a feast day are mutually exclusive. We also mean that work is an everyday occurrence, while a feast is something special, unusual, an interruption in the ordinary passage of time. Apparently the festive quality of a holiday depends upon its being exceptional. A festival can arise only out of the foundation of a life whose ordinary shape is given by the working day. The do-nothing members of an idle rich class are hard put to it even to amuse themselves, let alone to celebrate a festival. The *dolce vita* is a desperately unfestive affair. There is, incidentally, considerable testimony that this sad truth applied also to the courtly festivals of the Baroque period, which many an innocent historian has described as highly festive occasions. The probability is that they sprang not from the joy of living, but from fear, from *horror vacui*, because the true prerequisite for festivity was lacking at these courts. They had "no everyday life and no work, nothing but time on their hands and boredom."

But of course a feast day is not sufficiently characterized by calling it a day of rest from work. This conception itself means more than the mere fact of non-working. It means that, quite contrary to the usual case, man does not care for what is useful, that is to say, for what has a purpose outside itself (this belongs to the very definition of utility and usefulness; we do what is useful not for its own sake, but 'in order' to get or to avoid something else). Now, the old idea of 'rest from work' means to have at least the opportunity of doing something which is not useful for anything else, and which has no 'in order to,' but which is meaningful in itself. And what is such an activity like? What is a human activity that is meaningful in itself? These are questions we cannot answer unless we have a conception of man. For what is involved is the fulfilment of human life and the form in which this fulfilment is to take place. Inevitably, therefore, we find ourselves concerned with such ideas as 'the perfection of man,' 'eternal life,' 'bliss,' 'Paradise.' Now there is little point in learning what any individual thinks all on his own about such fundamental matters. In this realm we should be wary of originality. It is more rewarding to consider what the tradition of humanity's wisdom, into which the thought of whole generations has entered, has to tell us. And what do the Ancients tell us? They say, for instance, that the name for the utmost perfection to which man may attain, the fulfilment of his being, is *visio beatifica* (the seeing that confers bliss). This is to say that the absolutely perfect activity, the one which is completely meaningful in itself, takes place in the form of seeing; more precisely, that it is achieved in an awareness of the divine ground of the universe.

But eschatology alone is not the issue. The traditional wisdom does not speak only of the ultimate perfection of life on the other side of death. It speaks also of man as an earthly being appearing in history, and asserts that man by nature craves the appeasement of his yearnings through seeing; that in this present life also, the utmost happiness takes the form of contemplation. And indeed it is for contemplation that the feastday exists! The concept of festivity cannot be thought of without an element of contemplation. This accords completely with what ethnology and the history of culture and religion say. They say, for example (I am quoting Karl Kerény), that to celebrate a festival is equivalent to "becoming contemplative and, in this state, directly confronting the higher realities on which the whole of existence rests."

Of course, the issues at stake here are extremely difficult and many-sided, but one thing is indisputable: anyone who is at a loss to say what activity is meaningful in itself, is also at a loss to say what a feast is. Not only the theoretical concept of festivity is in question, however. Much more at issue is the prerequisite for achieving any kind of festivity. With the death of the concept of human activity which is meaningful in itself, the possibility of any resistance to a totalitarian labouring society also perishes (and such a regime could very well be established even without concomitant political dictatorship). It then becomes a sheer impossibility to establish

6 What is a Feast?

and maintain an area of existence which is not preempted by work; for there is only a single justification for not working that will be acceptable even to one's own conscience; that is, dedication of leisure to something meaningful in itself. It is not only 'socially' more important (as the usual saying goes), but it is also, on a higher human level, more dignified to work than to kill time; and if we contrast the labouring society and its totalitarian planning for utility with a civilization mainly dedicated to entertainment, the former seems without question overwhelmingly superior.

But the concept of the day of rest tells us something further about the essence of festivity. The day of rest is not just a neutral interval. It also entails a loss of utilitarian profit. In voluntarily keeping a holiday, men renounce the yield of a day's labour. A definite span of usable time is made, as the ancient Romans understood it, "the exclusive property of the gods." As the animal for sacrifice was once taken from the herd, so a piece of 'precious' available time is expressly withdrawn from utility. What happens is something like a free-will offering, something like a sacrifice. One could even say that what happens is almost like waste. And this unexpectedly brings us to a new aspect of festivity.

A festival is essentially a phenomenon of wealth; not, to be sure, the wealth of money, but of existential richness. At any rate, absence of calculation, in fact lavishness, is one of the elements of festivity. Of course there is a natural peril and a germ of degeneration inherent in this: the product of a whole year's labour can be senselessly and excessively thrown away on a single day. As is well known, men are quite capable of such behaviour, but this potential perversion cannot be included within the definition of festivity, as has recently been done. Nevertheless, the fact remains that the predominance of a calculating, economizing mentality prevents both festive excess and festivity itself. In the workaday world all magnificence and pomp is calculated, and therefore unfestive. The myriad lights of a commercialized Christmas remain a basically meagre display without any real radiance. You probably remember G. K. Chesterton's keen comment on the dazzling advertisements of Times Square at night: "What a glorious sight for those who luckily do not know how to read (to read of shaving cream or tooth paste)."

A day of non-working, of rest from work, of contemplation; a prepared span of time wherein may unfold an activity that is meaningful in itself; a time of non-calculation, of wealth, of superfluity, of waste–all this is true; but the heart of the matter, the essential thing which people have in mind when speaking of a feastday, clearly has still not entered our considerations.

One could ask whether a feast, for the normal thinking human, is not just a day of joy? On a festival day people enjoy themselves. Nietzsche, who terms it quite a 'trick' to find such people, is in fact saying exactly the same thing. And an early Greek Christian went so far as to say that festivity is joy and nothing else. Well, but joy at what? It is the nature of joy to be a secondary phenomenon. No one can rejoice 'absolutely,' for joy's sake alone. To be sure, it is foolish to ask a man why he wants to rejoice; to that extent joy is an end in itself. Nevertheless the longing for joy is nothing but the desire to have a reason for joy. This reason precedes joy and is different from it. The reason comes first; the joy comes second. (For the time being, I am not able nor do I wish to make up my mind to consent to Julian Huxley's strange idea that electric stimulation of a particular area in the brain can produce happiness, and that, as he says, "electric happiness is still happiness"–which leads us into the midst of his brother's *Brave New World*.) For true human happiness and joy, I think, there ought to be not only a cause, but a reason.

This reason for joy may be encountered in a thousand concrete forms. Nevertheless it consists always of the same thing: the possession or receiving of that which one loves, whether actually in the present, hoped for in the future, or remembered in the past. Joy is an expression of love. One who loves nothing and nobody cannot possibly rejoice, no matter how desperately he craves joy. Joy is the response of a lover upon receiving what he loves.

True as it is that a real festival cannot be conceived of without joy, it is no less true that first there must be a substantial reason for joy, which might also be called the festive occasion. This may even pass for the inner structure of a real feast, as Chrysostom has stated it in the clearest and tersest possible fashion: *Ubi caritas gaudet, ibi est festivitas* (where love rejoices, there is festivity).

But the question is still open: what sort of reason underlies festal joy and therefore festivity itself? Very different answers have been given to this question! One goes like this: "Plant a flower-decked pole in the middle of an open place, call the people together–and you have a feast." Everybody, one would think, can see that that is not enough. Yet this sentence is not an invention of mine, in order to give an example of naive simplification. No, it was written by Jean Jacques Rousseau.

It is an almost equally hopeless simplification to imagine that mere ideas can be the occasion for real festivals. It is scarcely surprising that no response was forthcoming when Easter was declared a festival of 'immortality,' not to speak of such fantastic proposals as those of Auguste Comte, whose reformed calendar established festivals of Humanity, Paternity and even Domesticity. Not even the idea of freedom can inspire people to celebrate a feast, though the event of liberation might, assuming that this event, though possibly belonging to the distant past, still has compelling contemporary force. Memorial days are not in themselves festival days. Strictly speaking, the past cannot be celebrated festively. If the Incarnation of God is no longer understood as an event that directly concerns the present lives of men, it becomes impossible, even absurd, to celebrate Christmas festively.

Josef Andreas Jungmann has recently suggested that festivals as an institution have already become derivative, whereas the prototypal form of festival still takes place where a specific event such as birth, marriage or homecoming is being directly celebrated. This sounds rather plausible, but if the implication is that the specific is the real and the whole reason of celebration, then the thesis is not altogether convincing. Can we festively celebrate the birth of a child if we hold with Jean Paul Sartre's dictum, "It is absurd that we are born"? I suggest that

10 What is a Feast?

anyone who is seriously convinced of this can no more celebrate the birth of his child than any other birthday, whether his own or someone else's, a fiftieth, or sixtieth, or any other. No single specific event can become the occasion for festive celebrations unless—unless what?

Here, at this very point, is where we must be able to name the reason underlying all others, the 'reason why' events such as birth, marriage, and homecoming can be experienced as the receiving of something beloved, without which there can be neither joy nor festivity. Again we find Nietzsche expressing the crucial insight. It is to be found in his posthumous notes, and reads: "To have joy in anything one must approve everything." That is to say, underlying all festive joy kindled by a specific circumstance there has to be an absolutely universal affirmation extending to the world as a whole, to the reality of things and the existence of man himself: everything, that is, is good, and it is good to exist. (Need we bother to say how little such affirmation has to do with shallow optimism, let alone with smug approval of that which in fact is?) Such affirmation may be performed with tears, and it even proves its seriousness by its confrontation with historical evil; whereas, on the other hand, whoever refuses assent to reality as a whole, no matter how well off he may be, is by that fact incapacitated for either joy or festivity. Festivity is impossible to the nay-sayer. The more money he has, and above all, the more leisure, the more desperate is this impossibility to him. This is also true of the man who refuses to approve his own existence, having fallen into that mysterious "despair from weakness" of which Kierkegaard has spoken and which

What is a Feast?

in the old moral philosophy went by the name of *acedia* (slothfulness of the heart). At issue is a refusal regarding the very heart and fountainhead of existence itself, because the "despair of not willing to be oneself" makes man unable to live with himself. He is driven out of his own house into the hurly-burly of work-and-nothing-else, into the fine-spun exhausting game of sophistical phrase-mongering, into 'incessant entertainment' aided by empty stimulants–in short, into a no-man's land which may be quite comfortably furnished, but which has no peace for the serenity of real leisure or for contemplation, and certainly not for festivity.

Festivity lives on affirmation.

Even celebrations for the dead, All Souls and Good Friday, can never be truly celebrated except on the basis of the conviction that there is consolation, for consolation is a form of joy and rejoicing, although the most silent of all; just as catharsis, the purification of the soul in the witnessing of tragedy, is at bottom a joyful experience.

Strictly speaking, however, it is insufficient to call affirmation of the world a mere prerequisite and premise for festivity. In fact it is far more. It is the substance of festivity itself. Festivity in its essential core is nothing but the living out of this affirmation. To celebrate a festival means to live out, for some special occasion and in an uncommon manner, the universal assent to the world as a whole. This statement, which may even be taken as a kind of definition, harmonizes with the conclusions cultural and religious historians have drawn from their studies of the great typical festivals in ancient cultures and among primitive peoples. And because that assent to life, if it is there at all, is there all the time, it becomes the well-spring of a thousand legitimate occasions for festivity, whether the immediate event be the coming of spring or of a baby's first tooth.

This is the point at which we must state explicitly a conclusion toward which all our foregoing ideas have inexorably led. To be sure, as I have found time and again, this conclusion is usually greeted with some distrust. But I see no legitimate way of avoiding it. It is absolutely compelling, both logically and existentially. The conclusion is divisible into several parts. First, there can be no more radical assent to the world than the praise of God, the lauding of the Creator of this same world. Second, the ritual praise in public worship is the most festive form that festivity can possibly take. Third, there can be no deadlier, more ruthless destruction of festivity than to refuse ritual praise.

These statements are, as I know, open to countless possible misunderstandings. For instance, to say that the ritual festival is the most festive of festivities—do we mean that there can be no secular, worldly festivals? Of course not! But the matter is rather complicated, and a simple answer will not suffice.

On the one hand, real festivity cannot be restricted to any one particular sphere of life, neither to the religious nor to any other. It seizes and permeates all dimensions of existence. Until I was eight years old, I thought that Whitsunday simply meant country fair, because our village would 'celebrate' both the same day. Or take the Corpus Christi Day in Toledo, Spain: the streets, canopied with canvas, are transformed into a vast festive tent whose walls are formed by the tapestry-decked facades of the houses, and whose floor is strewn with rosemary and lavender, which give out a stronger perfume the more they are walked on. High Mass in the Cathedral is followed by the procession, which is simultaneously a musical performance, a military parade, a social display, and, of course, Exposition and Escort of the Sacrament. The bullfight in the afternoon–how could it be less secular than at other times? But it is the Corrida del Corpus. Wherever festivity can freely vent itself in all its possible forms, an event is produced which leaves no zone of life, worldly or spiritual, untouched.

But now we must consider the 'on the other hand.' There are worldly, but there are no purely profane festivals, and we may presume not only that we can not find them, but also that they can not exist. A festival without gods–that is a non-concept, is inconceivable. For example, Mardi Gras remains festive only where Ash Wednesday still exists. To eliminate Ash Wednesday is to eliminate Mardi Gras itself. Yet Ash Wednesday is obviously nothing but a day in Christendom's liturgical year.

Thus secular as well as religious festivals have their roots in ritual worship. Otherwise what arises is by no means a profane festival, but either a new and more strenuous kind of work or just an embarrassment, something quite artificial. To be sure, what does 'artificial' mean? It is certainly true that all festivals are in one sense man-made, not only celebrated but also instituted by men. Almost everything about festivals, including the great and traditional ones, is indubitably the result of human arrangements, from the fixing of a particular calendar day to the specific forms of sacrifices, the ceremonies, the parades, and so on. Human institutions, then. Nevertheless the Biblical sentence, which by the way recurs in Plato's dialogues, remains absolutely valid: the festival is a day "the Lord has made." It remains true because while man can make the celebration, he cannot make what is to be celebrated, cannot make the festive occasion, the reason for celebrating; for example, the happiness of being created, *donum creationis*, which Thomas Aquinas considers to be the festive occasion of the Seventh Day, Sunday, on which creation was finished and approved by the Creator. (In India, while attending some of the great festivals, I asked people here and there, "What is the reason for your festive joy?" and an educated orthodox Hindu answered, "It is the joy of being a creature whom God has created out of joy")–but I must take up the thread of my unfinished statement. The happiness of being created, the existential goodness of things, the participation in the life of God, the overcoming of death, all these occasions of the great traditional festivals are pure gift. And because no one can confer a gift on himself, something that is entirely a human institution cannot be a real festival.

On the other hand, wherever in the course of history we encounter artificial holidays, we may conclude that they point to a particular interpretation of man's being: to the claim that man, especially in the exercise of political power, is able to bring about his own salvation as well as that of the world. Proof of such lofty powers can always be simulated, provided political propaganda tries hard enough. The semblance can even be kept up, at any rate for a while. And on the basis of such 'proof,' artificial festivals, for a time at least, can thrive and even exert a more or less convincing spell, especially if the combined powers of pseudo-arts, entertainment, sensationalism and manipulated illusion are brought to bear, and if, in addition, the political rulers command and control such 'spontaneous festive gladness.'

But it makes little sense to describe in abstract terms the counterpart of the true festival. Indeed, it is not necessary, for we can encounter it within our own history, probably for the first time in some specific establishments of the French Revolution which were intended to oust and replace the traditional religious feasts of Christendom. The results of these attempts are altogether forgotten, having fallen into absolute oblivion. Contemporary accounts speak of boredom, the infinite boredom of utter unreality, which makes the reading of them a startling experience. The extravagant expenditure on pinchbeck symbolical properties, on plaster, cardboard and tin, the bombastic declamations of platitudes, the empty histrionics of the pseudo-liturgy exude a feeling of empty illusion when we read, for instance, that the mayor of Paris displayed the book containing the Constitution from the altar of the Motherland, holding it out to his fellow citizens like a monstrance. Or that a girl ignited a Bengal light by means of a magnifying glass, producing a 'holy fire' which then flared up from a Greek vase in the hues of the Tricolor. Or that the important 'Festival of the Supreme Being' was founded by Robespierre, and celebrated for the first time on June 8, 1794, staged by Jacques Louis David, with the 'liturgist' of the ceremonies being Robespierre in person. Thus, at the conclusion of a speech at the Tuilleries, he ordered a mighty statue of Atheism, constructed of inflammable material, to be set afire. The flames were to reveal an equally enormous statue of Wisdom. At last a hymn was sung, the last stanza in chorus. "Simultaneously"–I am quoting now the account of the *Moniteur*–"the girls tossed flowers on high; the young men drew their swords and swore to make their weapons victorious everywhere. The old men placed their hands on the young men's heads and gave them their paternal blessing. Finally, a detachment of artillery (the arm of national vengeance) fired into the air, and all citizens, expressing their feelings in fraternal embraces, ended the festival with the resounding cry of humanity and civic conscience, 'Long live the Republic!'" "A tragic operetta," all this has been called. But such epithets do not do justice to the true evil and hopelessness of this lustily celebrated nonsense.

More characteristic perhaps of the new festivals than their empty theatrical pose was their coercive nature. Those who did not participate made themselves suspect. Several days beforehand, the citizen could read in the newspaper what was expected of him (I am again quoting the *Moniteur*): "When the bells ring all will leave their houses, which will be entrusted to the protection of the law and Republican virtues. The populace will fill the streets and public squares, aflame with joy and fraternity"–and so on. Naturally that sort of thing is not a gentle appeal for the friendly co-operation of the public; it is an edict. Thenceforth the element of political coercion and propagandistic intimidation became an essential part of the artificial festival, and this led inevitably to a pervasive, constitutional dishonesty, which ever since has been another of the characteristic signs of the artificial holiday. There is no way to tell whether participation in them is a measure of self-protection because not to participate would be politically dangerous, or whether it is a conditioned response to the deafening blare of a propaganda machine that has taken over every agency of communication. Even the participant himself can scarcely say how he 'really' feels about it, which may sound incredible, although not to those who know ideologically based despotism from the inside.

Yet we cannot say that the French Revolution as a historical event ushered in the obverse of true festivity. The unrealistic extravagance of these *fêtes*, their bombast and enthusiasm, are evidence that the society which launched them had not arrived at the purest form of rationally calculated utility. Only when that point is reached can we say that festivity itself, and not just a particular variety of festivity, has been negated in principle. This negation was reserved for a later, more consistent age in which the "transformation of the individual into the worker" would be completed, and the romantic notion of the "priests of social felicity" contained in the pamphlets of the French Revolution could be supplanted by the more brutal standard of the "social engineer."

When the American Federation of Labour decided to set May 1, 1886, as the target date for winning the eight-hour day which it had been demanding for years, the only thing in favour of the first of May was that it was moving day, the usual day when leases and other economic agreements ran out. There was no talk of mythical 'spring festivals' or other ideas rooted in folklore. The employers, as you know, rejected the demand, and so a strike was called for that day. At a demonstration in Chicago a bomb was thrown. The police fired into the crowd. Several of the demonstrators were killed, many wounded. Then came a trial in a problematic atmosphere. Seven labour leaders were sentenced to death, four actually executed. In memory of all this, the first of May was adopted internationally as a day given over to demonstrating for shorter working hours. And then, five years later, the International Labor Congress in Brussels declared it a 'festival day' for the first time. But herewith something quite new was started, with unforseeable consequences which ultimately caused the historical occasion to be completely forgotten, and which were fully realized only in the May Day celebrations of totalitarian regimes. However, the posters and banners carried in the procession ("This is the day the people made," or "Socialism, thy Kingdom come!"), as well as the propaganda pamphlets and leaflets distributed in honor of the 'festival,' proclaimed from the beginning the purpose of displacing the traditional festivals of Christendom, which were rejected as bourgeois institutions.

Once again it must be said that all this was a more or less innocent prelude to what was to come. The situation became serious when the Bolshevist regime took over the 'socialist holiday,' for the day could then no longer retain its character of a demonstration against the established order: the established order had become identical with the dictatorship of the proletariat. What, then, was to be done with the first of May? It was turned into something quite unexpected, though unexpected only to those who do not have an adequate conception of the nature of the totalitarian labour state. The first of May became, to put it briefly, a day that differed from all other workdays and restdays of the year in that it was celebrated by- additional, voluntary, unpaid work! Maxim Gorki said: "It is a wonderful idea to make the spring festival of the workers a holiday of voluntary work." The "rehearsal for the general strike" (as Aristide Briand had called the first of May) was forgotten; on the contrary, Leon Trotzky said, "This holiday is one of general work." Naturally the 'voluntary' nature of this strange holiday work must be understood in a propaganda sense. One must not fail to hear the overtones of a threat. Gorki even ruled it a crime not to understand the purpose of giving that particular form to the holiday, and the phrase 'labor deserter' began to be bandied about.

That heroic effort of 1920 was not sustained, by the way. Instead, still another meaning, again a very characteristic one, soon came to the fore. From about 1922 on, May first became more and more exclusively a day on which the Soviet Union displayed its military strength. What Mademoiselle de Scudéry had said in regard to the Baroque festivals came to apply here too: the celebration served chiefly to demonstrate the 'grandeur' of its sponsors.

In this atmosphere the gigantic May Day celebrations of the Nazi regime flourished. Their coercive character became even more obvious. There were not many persons in Germany who could afford to stay away from the parades, and it is not at all surprising that, according to the official propaganda instructions, German cities, large and small, could scarcely be distinguished on that day from Italian or Spanish cities decorated for Corpus Christi Day or for the festival of a saint. The only reality hidden behind the bombast and empty spectacle was, just as in the Soviet state, the total subjection of human beings to work. And then the same shift in meaning took place once again. In National Socialist Germany, May first became the prime occasion for striking displays of weapons of destruction, which the regime was already accumulating in preparation for total war.

At this point a terrifying conclusion must be drawn from all this: the artificial holiday is not only a sham festival; it borders so dangerously on counterfestivity that it can abruptly be reversed into something that should perhaps be called an 'anti-festival.'

Roger Caillois, a French historian of culture and one of the very few writers who have expressly tried to elaborate something like a theory of festivity, tells us that one day he asked himself what nowadays takes that place in the life of society which formerly was filled by the great festivals. At first, he says, he imagined that the answer might be vacations. But then he realized that in the present world it is instead war that fulfills the functions of the great festivals. In war, he says, all the attributes of festivals may be found (he considers festivals as essentially 'a time of excess'): the most drastic conversion and consumption of energies, the eruption of stored force, the merging of the individual in the totality, the squandering of resources ordinarily carefully husbanded, the wild breaking down of inhibitions, and so on. "C'est la guerre qui correspond à la fête."

Once we have recovered from the shock and begin casting about for counterarguments, we are forced to admit, however much against our will, that such an extreme hypothesis is not entirely 'out of this world.' Since the time of Nietzsche, who called himself "the destroyer par excellence," and who dreamed of a company of men who would wish to be called destroyers –for almost three generations, then–the idea of "active nihilism," of the "will to nothingness" and "pleasure even in destruction" has been an element in the modern attitude toward life. Even Pierre Teilhard de Chardin, although enthusiastically convinced of the future energy of the Cosmos, feels called upon to speak of a dawning "organic crisis in evolution" and of the "threat of strikes in the noosphere;" more precisely, he says, "there is a danger that the world may refuse itself when perceiving itself through reflection."

Evidently this strike has already begun. "Darkening of the world," "flight of the gods," "disintegration of reality," "absurdity of existence," "nausea"–such are the key words heard on every hand, whether in philosophical or literary discussions, whether the subject be visual arts or music. He who laughs has not yet received the terrible tidings, as Bertolt Brecht says.

Now it is just a matter of time before those negations, reaching a certain degree of intensity, render true festivity impossible. At the same time–this seems considerably less self-evident–they pave the way for something else: a new feeling that the destruction of the world, for example in a global war of annihilation, is no longer to be feared as an unspeakable calamity, but anticipated as something to be desired, even 'celebrated' as ordinarily only affirmations can be, celebrated as an anti-festival, as one of those great 'uprisings' which again Kurt Eisner has described as borrowing "the means from war and the mood from festivals."

To shut our eyes to the possibility of such a development would mean repressing a whole dimension of reality. This, too, lies within the nature of man as a historical being. I really do not know how an incorruptible mind, faced with the evil in the world, could keep from utter despair, were it not for the conviction that there is a divinely guaranteed goodness of being which no amount of mischief can undermine. Perhaps it is only thanks to such super-empirical certainties that man is able to assume the intellectually and existentially extremely demanding task of facing naked reality without resorting to the evasions either of euphemism or of slander. What ultimately counts is truth. And might it not be the truth that the man who despairs, he in particular has "not yet received" certain tidings?

On the other hand, whoever has received and accepted them knows at the same time that the core and source of festivity remain inviolably present in the midst of society, today as a thousand years ago. It remains in the form of the praise given in ritual worship, which is literally performed at every hour of the day. 'The' festive occasion pure and simple, the divine guarantee of the world and of human salvation, exists and remains true continuously. In the light of this conviction, the empirically patent unfestivity of the contemporary world appears as something not altogether hopeless. It is, however, a condition which is difficult to decipher and, above all, a condition which is in suspense, a condition which involves and conceals and leaves open the extreme historical potentialities, among them the most radical celebration of the antifestival.

Hope and History

In the last decade of the eighteenth century, which means in the decade of the French Revolution, somebody asked the question "whether the Human Race is continually advancing towards the Better." This 'somebody' was Immanuel Kant, seventy years old at the time. Abstractly speaking, there are, he says, three possible answers to this question, and no decision has yet been reached, or so it seems. The first answer is yes, we are going up-hill; the second answer is no, we are going down; and the third answer is that history takes its course more or less on the same level. Now one of these possible answers is immediately eliminated by Kant without any discussion: the second answer, retrogression to the worse. This is simply inconceivable for Kant. Why? Because, he says, this would imply that the human race might "blot itself out;" and just this is, for the man of the eighteenth century, an obviously unthinkable idea. Exactly the same representation, on the contrary, has become for the man of the modern epoch not only thinkable and discussable, but immediately acute. "Man's existence now, and for the first time, is threatened"–that is the first statement of a paper given at the London Symposium on Man and his Future (1962). And of course the most striking argument is the actual destructibility of man by his own weapons. This has been said many times in the historical and philosophical literature of recent years. To quote Karl Jaspers: "The situation is irrevocable: man is able to put out mankind and all life on earth by his own action; and mere reason tells him that this end will likely come in the near future." Another diagnosis is summarized this way: "We are the first men to master the Apocalypse." Although this phrase, 'mastering the Apocalypse,' is rather unfortunate, the meaning is quite clear.

This knowledge immediately gives us such a superiority over the man of the eighteenth century (after all, Kierkegaard is not entirely wrong when he says, "He who has been deceived is wiser than he who has not been deceived") that it might not seem very fair to debate on this matter with Kant. Was he not simply unable to imagine that the self-destruction of man could be even technically possible? True, but the nature of historical man has not changed since Kant, even since Adam, or should I say since Cain? By the way, in the last paragraph I used the term 'modern epoch.' Epoch sounds all too deceptively like a long duration, and it may give the likewise deceptive impression of neutral academic distance. It rather obscures the explosiveness of our situation, which may change suddenly from one moment to the next into the catastrophe. "Nobody will," as Konrad Lorenz says, "predict a long life for man, when they look at him as he stands there–in his hands the H-bomb which he got as a gift of his reason, and in his heart the instinct of aggression which that same reason is unable to master." And as stated several times at the London Symposium already mentioned, "These are not long-term problems; they are upon us now."

It goes without saying that in this situation the topic "Hope and History" has an unprecedented urgency. But on what does the discussion centre, actually and exactly? The problem "Hope and History" may indeed be viewed from several perspectives. I should like to mention only two of them. First, does it or does it not belong to the nature of human hope to reach its fulfilment in the field of history? Can what man is hoping for possibly be realized within history? Second, does the course of human history actually foster and encourage the hope of man? Or to put it otherwise, is it possible, without any intellectual dishonesty, not to despair when looking at human history?

Before going into any further discussion, we must state as clearly as possible what we understand by "hope," and what by "history." What then do people mean whenever they speak of hope and hoping? The first element is certainly expectation. But I can expect something for which I do not hope, and I can also expect something indifferent and irrelevant or even something terrible. I speak of hope only where my longing and my desire are involved; I hope only for something good ('good' in the very broad sense of the word, ranging from 'good weather,' to 'how good that you came!'). Yet longing and desire alone do not make hope. I may yearn after something which I know I shall never get, which means, after something that I am not really hoping for. Hope implies confidence and even a kind of certainty. Of course, there is also futile hope, and there are hopes that are disappointed at the last. But in the very moment in which I become sure of the fruitlessness of my hope, I cease hoping. This, by the way, is the reason why joy belongs, if not to the essence of hope, then to its permanent company. Hope aims at the attainment of what we love, and therefore it cannot be without joy. In a German philosophical dictionary I found as a first description of hope, *freudige Erwartung* (joyful expectation). This is certainly very much to the point, although it is far from a complete characterization of what everybody means by hope. It may well be that I am expecting something desired and something wished-for with confidence and joy, and yet that nobody would speak of my expectation as hope. There is a famous German poem which begins, "Come, peaceful night, world's comfort, come...." I might quite possibly say this from the depth of my heart, but of course it would be nonsense to speak of hope here. Nobody hopes for the nightfall. I cannot hope for something that will happen anyway, inevitably. This statement, by the way, has some consequences. If it is really true that the classless society is coming with the necessity of a law of nature, then *eo ipso* it can not be an object of human hope. To repeat: whatever will happen anyway, and whatever is attainable easily, without much trouble, cannot really be objects of human hope.

The Ancients spoke of the *bonum arduum*, the "steep good," referring to something which does not lie within hand's reach, to something that one may fail to get. At this point appears yet another element of the concept of hope: the object of hope is not at the disposal of the hoping man. Nobody hopes for something which he is able to make or procure for himself; in such a case we do not speak of hope. We need only to have a look at everyday usage: I hope the train will arrive on time; let us hope the weather will be fine tomorrow; it is to be hoped that our friend will regain his health; we hope that there will be no World War III; and so on. One thing is completely clear in all these phrases. We do not control that for which we hope. If an artist who is about to transform his idea into a corporeal work of stone or wood or perhaps verse, says, "I hope I shall succeed in doing so," then he is expressing, quite correctly, the fact that this does not depend on himself alone. Or when a carpenter tells me, "I hope the desk or the bookrack will be delivered within the fixed time," he expresses, again quite correctly, that he is depending on several circumstances and other people outside his range of influence. I should like to extend this example a bit. If this same craftsman, after a long talk on the very special shape of that desk or bookrack, should tell me, "I hope I shall succeed in making the desk exactly according to our outline," well, I think I had better find another carpenter, since nobody speaks of hope at all, if he is really able to make something by himself. A father may say to his high school boy, "I hope you will be much more diligent next year," but if the boy should answer, "That is what I am hoping for, too," it would be just plucky nonsense. All of which leads to one rather serious point (I am quoting Gabriel Marcel): "The only genuine hope is directed to something that does not depend on ourselves." This statement again has some consequences. One consequence sounds like this. If, as Friedrich Engels said, man himself is really the maker of history (of course, in a limited sense this is quite correct, but if Engels' statement is meant to be a complete description of the fact in question), it immediately becomes meaningless to connect the concepts of hope and history.

Human language, however, spoken and understood by everybody, has some other perhaps unexpected insights. In Plato's *Symposium*, Diotima speaks of the strange phenomenon whereby, although there are many makers, only one maker is called simply the maker, *poietēs*, the poet. In the linguistic field of love, she continues, there are many kinds of love: love of parents, love of friends, love of one's native country and so on; but if you speak simply of lovers, you do not mean those who love their country or their parents; you mean those who love in the sense of Eros. And I think that again something similar comes true in the case of hope. Countless different things, from fine weather for a vacation to peace in the world, can be the objects of hope, and in fact are. Nevertheless, there seems to be only one object, the hope for which makes a man simply and, so to speak, absolutely hopeful. Perhaps the inverse side may make things clearer. There are a thousand hopes which a man may give up, and which may be dashed or buried, without that man's becoming necessarily hopeless in the absolute sense. Yet clearly there is only one single hope, the loss of which would make a man plainly hopeless, purely destitute of hope. The question is, what sort of hope is this? What hope must a man have lost, so that it might rightly be said, he is simply without hope and plainly hopeless?

In order to be able to answer or even to discuss this question adequately, we must consider a distinction for which neither the English nor the German language has the terms, in contrast with the French language, which distinguishes between *espoir* and *espérance*. A German philosopher suggests distinguishing between hope (singular) and hopes (plural), which seems to serve quite well. The enormous relevance of the underlying distinction, however it may be named, comes to light in the findings of modern medical psychology. I am speaking of the very exact phenomenological investigations which have been made in recent years in the University Hospital of Heidelberg by Professor Herbert Plügge (*Wohlbefinden und Missbefinden*, Tuebingen, 1962). For years Plügge has concerned himself with the inner situation of people for whom hope has been challenged in a very decisive way, namely with the situation of incurables, of people who have just learned that they are incurably ill; and also with the inner condition of people who have tried to commit suicide. In the course of this purely empirical investigation Herbert Plügge caught sight, as he says, of a quite different hope, different from what he calls the ordinary, common and everyday hopes (again plural!). The new hope is singular. Plügge calls it the fundamental and the genuine hope. Ordinary hopes are directed towards an object that belongs to the world, towards something which we are expecting from somewhere else, towards some news or success or bodily health, whereas the fundamental hope has no object of this kind. You cannot point at it with your finger, and it is rather difficult to describe it. Moreover, the fundamental hope seems to come about only if the ordinary hopes are disappointed. Of course, the hope (singular) also has an object. Plügge says this object does not belong to those things that man can 'have'; it has to do with what man himself 'is.' The object is self-realization in the future, or personal wholeness.

One main point, however, is that (I am quoting Herbert Plügge) "the genuine hope comes into existence out of the loss of the ordinary hopes." Disappointment here means to become free from, and to get rid of, an illusion. The illusion which perhaps nobody is able to avoid from the beginning consists in the belief that wholeness of existence implies the attainment of certain material goods, including bodily health. The disappointment of this belief all of a sudden enables us to realize what perhaps we knew 'theoretically'; namely, that not only does the true wholeness of man consist in something else, but also, that we ourselves are in fact hoping for this 'something else' with a much more vital and even with an invincible power of our soul. And yet, disappointment means not only the correction of an error. Plügge speaks of liberation. The definite experience of incurability, he says, makes possible "a freedom from the captivity of illness, which could not possibly be reached before the breakdown." The relevance of this finding, I think, goes far beyond the immediate topic of Plügge's investigation, although as to the deadly ending we are, by the way, all in the same position. Every deep disappointment of a hope which had been directed towards something within this world contains, as it seems, the chance that 'the' hope (singular) might turn without any resignation (this is important) to its true object, and that, in an act of liberation, a larger breathing space might

Hope and History   33

become open and enterable. It is precisely in the disappointment, and perhaps only in the disappointment, that we receive the invitation, which we are nevertheless not bound to follow, to enter this larger room of 'the' hope.

One may of course raise the question of whether 'the' hope, the fundamental hope, cannot perhaps itself be disappointed. Surprisingly, it looks as if the answer to this question actually has to be no, 'the' hope cannot be disappointed. Man may lose it, he may give it up or put it aside–which rightly should be called not disappointment but despair; but to be disappointed, to prove to be false, to come to nothing, to be broken off–all that can never happen to 'the' hope. And why not? Where is it written?

The answer, I think, should start from a clearer understanding of what disappointment means. It means the positive experience of fruitlessness and of non-fulfilment. Now this experience can never be made in the case of 'the' hope, because the time span of waiting for the event of fulfilment or non-fulfilment is exactly identical with the time span of life itself. Despair does not mean that the hope has actually been disappointed, but despair is the anticipation of such a disappointment. To despair means to anticipate the non-fulfilment. The moment in which the true result of human existence becomes manifest remains imminent precisely as long as that same existence lasts. There is not one moment in life in which a man, be he a hundred years old and be he at the threshold of death, can legitimately say, "Now I am no longer on the way, the fulfilment lies no longer in the future, I already possess whatever has been intended for me." To put it another way: man's existence itself has the structure of 'not yet.' I could also say, it has the structure of hope.

Now it is not hard to see that this hope-structure of man's existence has to do with his historicity; that is to say, with the quality by reason of which man is able to have history. History could even be called the field of man's hope (and hopes).

This is the point at which to be more precise about what we understand by 'history.' The German word *Geschichte* is derived from *geschehen*, which means "to happen;" history is that which happens. But apparently not all that happens is history. There are also non-historical happenings. The flow of water, the flash of lightning, the turn of the tide—none of these are history. It has been said that events, even such natural events as these, become strictly historical as soon as they bear some relation to man. This is true to some extent. However, not all that happens to a man automatically makes up his history. That we are born, that we grow up, that we get old, that we die, is not, strictly speaking, our history. Not even what comes to us in our lifetime, whether this be a person (a teacher, a loved one, an adversary), or the loss or gain of fortune, health, or beauty, or even natural attributes (talents, temper, strength or weakness), can properly be called our history. Our history is the record of what we make of all this. It is the combination of what happens and of what we ourselves do. An event becomes a strictly historical event whenever freedom, responsibility, decision, and also the possibility of guilt and misdeed come into play.

This again is the reason why historical events cannot be deduced or calculated, why they cannot be derived from what is known already. This, in part, constitutes the difference between history and evolution, and I should say that just this difference is in danger of being obscured and forgotten in contemporary discussions. Yet it is exactly this difference which is important with regard to hope. Expressed as an abbreviated formula, it could be said that hope and evolution present no problem; the problem is hope and history.

I once had the honour of having among my listeners Pierre Teilhard de Chardin, at a lecture given in Paris in 1951. Unfortunately I did not know it at that time. I only learned of it ten years later, and I learned at the same time, that Teilhard de Chardin passionately refused my thesis. My topic was *L'espérance des martyrs* ("The Hope of the Martyrs"), and I was especially anxious to make one thing clear: that it is not worthwhile to speak of human hope at all, if there is no hope left to the martyr; that is, to him whose innerworldly hopes have become altogether groundless, and who, in the common meaning of the word, is in a hopeless situation–in a concentration camp, about to be executed, left alone, ridiculed–and so on. I did not suppress either that it is nowhere written that the situation of the martyr must be an exceptional situation, which may take place here and there, but generally in remote times and countries. Teilhard, as I said, declined vehemently as defeatism even the way of putting the whole question. The decisive point is quite a different one, says Teilhard (in a letter published later on in his biography). The decisive question is whether man has, biocosmically (*biocosmiquement*), a right to hope beyond all sentimentality, philosophy and mysticism. The decisive point is that mankind is, considering its evolutionary potential, objectively young and full of future and therefore entitled to hope.

Now this is exactly what I call confounding history and evolution. Of course there is evolution (that is the development and unfolding of what was before still enveloped and folded), and this occurs also in the realm of the specifically human, even in the realm of intellectual life! In the earliest grasping of pre-historical man at the powers of nature, and in the very first use of any energy of the material cosmos, there was something still undeveloped, which since then has consistently and even to some degree automatically unfolded over man's head, up to the conquest of atomic energy. And there is no doubt at all that mankind will develop and improve immensely all its achievements in this field. As far as the possibility of progress is concerned we may look forward to the time to come with composure, confidence and hope. Also with hope? At this point we hesitate. In fact we are not at all confident, nor hopeful and calm, when, for instance, facing the increasing sophistication of nuclear weapons. And this nervousness has its reason in something quite different from any disbelief in the evolutionary potential of human technological intelligence. It has its reason in the anxiety concerning what man, as a moral being, may actually do with this immeasurable power, and for what purpose he may use it. In Bertolt Brecht's play *Galileo*, Galileo says: "You may gradually discover whatever can be discovered. But one day... it might happen that your cheers for a new achievement will be answered by a universal cry of horror."

At this point, I think, the difference between history and evolution becomes absolutely obvious. In Teilhard's main work, *The Phenomenon of Man*, there is one sentence in which both aspects are connected. I quote: "If Mankind... makes use of its immeasurable remaining time of life, it has inexhaustible possibilities ahead of it." Now, the potential of immeasurable possibilities (mankind is still young!)–this is the aspect of evolution! On the other hand, the 'if' (if mankind makes use of its possibilities)–this is the aspect of history! But what actually happens and what will happen, that will be decided not in the field of evolution but in the field of history. And nothing but this is of immediate concern to us. This is a question of life and death. After all, the question of the biological potential of mankind does not rob us of sleep, but the question of our historical future does. We are always about to ask this question. At the same time, however, it is clear that there is an enormous difference with regard to the answerability of the two questions. It might be quite possible to find out scientifically whether mankind as a species is still young, but how should it be made possible to find out whether mankind, however young, will one day eradicate itself? Here freedom and decision are in play, and that is why there never will be any calculable certainty about man's historical future, even if the methods of statistical prognostication are perfected. Certainly it would have been possible to predict rather exactly, some years in advance, how many fatal traffic accidents there would be in the city of Danzig

38 What is a Feast?

in April 1945, but that this very city of Danzig at that time actually did not exist any more, and that there was nothing at all like traffic there–this could not have been predicted, at least not on the basis of statistics. There is, in Pascal's *Pensees*, a remarkable aphorism; it is decipherable only if you consider the year in which it was written. The aphorism goes thus: "Could anyone enjoying the friendship of the King of England, the King of Poland and the Queen of Sweden have believed that he might be without refuge and asylum in the whole world?" The year–1656! This was the year of the deposition of the King of Poland. Two years earlier the Queen of Sweden had abdicated, and the King of England had been executed seven years previously. No refuge any more!

The truly historical event, concrete in every respect (when? where? who?; these alone are of interest to the man concerned!)–the historical event cannot be foreseen at all in prognostication. For this, a kind of prediction would be necessary which did not depend on the knowledge of any 'footholds' in the past or in the present, as all prognostication does; for the art of prognosis consists in discovering in the fund of experience itself pointers to the future. With this I have already given a kind of negative definition of prophecy, which is, if there is one at all, the only sort of prediction which could possibly grasp a future historical event. I have said that it belongs to the essence of history that it cannot be deduced from what has been before. Now prophecy, by its very definition, is a prediction which is independent of any knowledge of what has been before.

The question is whether there is any strictly prophetical information about the historical future. If not, then it is meaningless to make any conjectures on how history might go on or even how it might end.

This is the quite respectable reason for the deep mistrust with which we regard visions of the future proclaimed with more or less certainty in the realm of science, of philosophy, of social religions, and so on. Wherefrom should we know that the human race is in fact continually advancing to the Better? Wherefrom should anyone know that man's effort to change the world, socialistically or not, will actually bring about the Golden Age, the *regnum humanum*, the kingdom of liberty, and so on? Who really knows anything about it?

But this is only one scruple. The other doubt which comes to mind while one considers all those visionary expectations is even more to the point. It has to do quite directly with the topic of hope. In all those visions of the future, there is said not a single word about death. I do not speak here of any metaphysical theory of death. No, I am speaking of the very simple fact that we shall be dead before the Golden Age will have come. In the London Symposium of 1962 of which I have already spoken, Hilary Koprowski, professor of medical research at the University of Pennsylvania (upon closer inspection of the biographical appendix, you will notice that he is a Polish immigrant, bearing on his shoulders the burden of old Europe), ironically called into question all the optimistic planning which thrived excessively in the climate of that convention. He reminded his listeners of the fact of death, quoting e.e. cummings: "It is funny, you will be dead some day;" and he also quoted the old epitaph *Et in Arcadia Ego*, which does not mean "I too have been in Arcadia," but, "Even in Arcadia am I, Death!" I think he intended to ask, What about Arcadia and the Golden Age as long as there is something called Death?

"Salvation is vain–unless it delivers us from death." This is a sentence by Gabriel Marcel which I immediately understand and to which I subscribe, whereas I do not understand one single word of what Ernst Bloch has to say regarding this same point: that the certainty of class consciousness is "a herb against death." Of course, I have no expectation that death can ever be put out of the world. And, of course, I do not say that it would be absurd to hope as long as the hoping person has to die. (By the way, death does not happen to the universe, to society, to evolution, but exclusively to the individual person; and also hope is not borne by any other subject except, again, the individual person.) To repeat: I do not say that hope is meaningless as long as there is death, but I do maintain that no conception whatsoever of the future condition of mankind in which death and man's destination to die have simply been left out of account can ever seriously claim to be an object of human hope at all. Of course, I may cultivate some prognostic ideas of what people will do on this planet, let us say, two hundred years from now–for example, trips to the moon, pocket-sized electronic means of communication, an increase of ten or twenty years in the average life span– and I may get rightly enthusiastic at these results of human intelligence and courage. But how and in what sense could I set my hope on all that? All of that concerns me in so far as I am curious, prognostically interested, eager for knowledge, but it does not concern me in so far as I hope. The hoping person is not one who wants to know something; he is one who wants to receive something that is good, to partake of 'the' good.

Everybody knows the polemical phrase, "to feed people with hopes of the beyond." This phrase, which occurs a hundred times in Marxist literature and is not very far from the famous "opium for the people" expression, implies, as you know, the charge that one is diverting the attention of the exploited people from pushing through their just interests by telling them of the glory of Heaven. I do not say that this situation has never occurred, or that it may not happen again, but I insist on this: if those decidedly innerworldly pictures of the future simply leave out death and the other side of death, which means, the future impending over all of us, they themselves are a merely abstract and deceptive consolation, and, in an exact inversion of the usual phrase, it is they who call people's attention to something which indeed is absolutely 'beyond' their real life. The only future which has already begun is the life on the other side of death, as Karl Rahner has said. This does not at all mean that the earthly history of man and mankind does not concern the hoping individual. But it does mean that, for earthly history to concern my hope ('the' hope of mine), it has to be thought of in connection with my own destiny on the other side of death.

How then to conceive of the historical future of man? I have said that if there is no legitimate prophecy, nobody knows anything. Now Christians are convinced that such a strictly prophetical source of information on history does indeed exist. Among their sacred books there is, for instance, the *Apocalypse*. But a prophecy is not just a plain description of what will happen in the future. A prophecy does not deprive the time to come of its character of being really future; the future still remains unknown to us. John Henry Newman said, "The event is the true key to prophecy." On the other hand, there certainly is something which we really get to know by accepting a legitimate prophecy as truth.

But what is it that we get to know? First of all, we are confirmed in an insight which our own thinking is able to reach: that man's history will not come to its fulfilment by way of a continuous process of evolution. In the heart of universal history there also is the frontier of death which separates mankind from its own perfection. Even Teilhard de Chardin, although enthusiastically convinced of the absolute future of the universe, speaks of a point of dissolution (*point de dissociation*) through which the process of evolution must go in order to come to its perfection. Immanuel Kant, in his last years, speaks much more clearly and realistically to this point in his pondering essay on *The End of All Things*. This end, the essay begins, apparently has to be thought of by way of analogy with the death of the individual, which in the language of the devout (as he says, speaking without irony) is usually called a transition out of time into eternity. In this representation there is, Kant says, something horrible and at the same time inviting. This is the reason why man cannot cease turning his terrified eyes on it always anew. One thing again is, I think, altogether evident: this step out of time can never be imagined as a gradual continuous development, but rather as a kind of rupture and destruction—this again by analogy with human dying, which also looks more like destruction than like progress and fulfilment. If fulfilment and consummation really do take place through the breakdown and together with it, they happen not only latently, but in spite of all appearances. This is something which we in fact do believe of the 'good' human death as well as, above all, of that paradigmatic dying "in the fulness of time." No observer could have found out what in truth did happen here.

Whoever considers this may be prepared to accept a further and even more important message included in the Apocalyptic prophecy, and he will no longer be inclined to take it as something absurd, even if terrifying. The message is this: that human history within time (this is important!) will not end with the plain triumph of the true and the good nor with the clear victory of reason and justice, but with something which again may hardly be distinguished from a catastrophe—not a cosmic one, but a historical catastrophe, consisting in a gigantic pseudo-order upheld and guaranteed by political power, by a world-despotism of evil.

Although a modern mind taking notice of this may at first be inclined to rebel, in fact such a gloomy expectation is quite familiar to the historical thinking of our epoch. Friedrich Nietzsche, for instance, passionately interested in the topic 'future' (his main work, which was never completed, was originally to have been titled *What is Coming?*), copied in his notebook a quote of Baudelaire and gave it the heading "Further evolution of mankind." Baudelaire for his part speaks of an imminent "phantom of order" erected by the political power with the help of violent measures which "would make shudder our contemporary world, however stupid it may have become." Hermann Rauschning, former President of the Senate of Danzig and today a farmer somewhere in the United States, is a modern politician legitimated by an especially intimate knowledge of totalitarian regimes. Rauschning thinks it altogether possible that there might come a world civilization of materialistic enjoyment on the basis of progressing dehumanization and under a totalitarian monopoly of power held by a world-grand-inquisitor. The term grand-inquisitor calls to mind the name of another great European who likewise had a presentiment of what was to come: Dostoevski. And indeed, in his legend of the Grand Inquisitor we read the bewildering statement: "At the end they will come and lay down their freedom at our feet and say, 'Make us your slaves but do feed us!'" Perhaps I should also quote the fierce remark from the *Ungarbled Thoughts* of the Polish intellectual Stanislaus Lec: "I should have to laugh, if they hadn't finished the destruction of the world before the end of the world."

But our objective is not to discuss modern visions of the historical future. We are still asking what prophetic information might be attainable concerning the end of history. Of course, it would not have much meaning to try for a private interpretation of the *Apocalypse*. Instead we should find out what the scientific theology of today has to say on this point. It is true that modern theologians react rather reticently as soon as the question of the end of the world or even of the Antichrist comes up. "It is very little that can be said here," Karl Rahner says. But if we look a bit more closely at the little which modern theologians actually do say, we get a rather clear answer. The answer sounds like this (I am quoting modern theological handbooks and dictionaries, Catholic and Protestant): the antagonistic character of history will be intensified at the end; one must expect an extreme concentration of the energy of the evil, and a vehemence never known before in the fight against Christ and Christendom (and against all men of good will, as Thomas Aquinas said in the thirteenth century). The *potentia saecularis* of the Antichrist is called the strongest world power in history, and so on. This alarming message cannot, I think, be easily ignored. Its implications are certainly manifold, but one thing is again made unmistakably clear: it is impossible to think of the end of history as of the crowning and harmonic conclusion of an uninterrupted and continuous, though perhaps difficult and dialectic, advancement, although as Teilhard de Chardin rightly says this would be much more in harmony with 'the theory,' and certainly not only with the theory of evolution, but also of Marxism and of the idealistic philosophy of Progress.

The conception of history behind the *Apocalypse* is thoroughly different. This conception not only takes human freedom seriously, including the freedom to do evil, but also considers 'the evil one' to be a demonic power of history. Therefore conflict, frustration, failure, unadjustable discord and even catastrophe cannot be foreign to the essence of human history, not even in its normal course.

Nevertheless, this is certainly not the last word of the *Apocalypse*. The last word and the decisive message is, in spite of all: blissful ending beyond all expectation; triumph over evil; victory over death; drinking from the Source of life; resurrection; God's dwelling with men; New Heaven and New Earth (all these terms and images are taken from the *Apocalypse*). With all this there is apparently something said about hope, too. It is said that the true hope cannot be paralysed or even touched by man's being prepared for an innerworldly catastrophe, whether this end is called dying, martyrdom, defeat of the good, or world despotism of evil.

But now the two previous questions, both of them, come back in full force. Has it not been confirmed that human history is a desperate business? What reasons for hope can possibly be furnished by history? Does it really belong to the nature of human hope, of 'the' hope, that it can never be satisfied in the field of history?

This last question has indeed been answered. If this worldly human existence has altogether the structure of 'not yet,' and if man as a pilgrim is really on the way up to the moment of his death, this hope, identical with our existence itself, is either thoroughly absurd or it will find its final fulfilment on the other side of death, 'beyond' the here and now.

Nevertheless any blame stemming from a charge of secluded 'beyondness' would absolutely miss the point for several reasons. These reasons, however, can be made evident, I am afraid, only to Christians. This does not mean that there are no wrong ideas of hope among

Christians, especially wrong ideas of its 'beyondness.' But in such cases the Christians misunderstand themselves. Be that as it may, non-Christians might still be reasonably expected at least to take notice of the Christian arguments on this point.

First of all, it is not true, as Friedrich Engels and the Marxists maintain, that Christian hope aims at the perfection of a separate history of the Kingdom of God apart from 'real' history, which Christians allegedly declare to be meaningless. The opposite is true. It is precisely this worldly creation, the creation before our eyes, whose perfection we are expecting, albeit through death and catastrophe. The kingdom of God will be realized nowhere but in the midst of historical mankind. It is true that nobody can know what in fact 'resurrection' and 'New Earth' concretely mean, but what else could they mean, if not that not the least jot will ever be lost of anything that earthly and historically is good, true, beautiful, genuine, right, and so on? As Hans Ursvon Balthasar puts it in his essay on Solovjev, "World's harvest *will* certainly be brought in"–but, he continues, "not by mankind itself."

Above all–this is point two–Christians are convinced that the frontier of death between 'here' and 'yonder' has, in a certain sense, been overcome from the other side, namely by that event which is designated by the theological term *incarnation*.

One of the recurring symbols by which men have tried to make clear to themselves the quintessence of what they are hoping for is the Great Banquet. Plato, too, speaks of it, and I think this should not be forgotten. He reminds us not only of the *synousia*, the common life of God and man on the other side of death, but he describes also the banquet in which the soul participates, outside of time and in a supercelestial place, as a guest and companion of the gods, satisfied by the contemplation of the highest being. The Christians could not say it much better, and indeed, they say it not very differently. But Plato for his part could not have had the least inkling of that community around God's table in which Christendom recognizes and celebrates the anticipation and the real beginning of the Great Banquet on the other side of death. From earliest times this anticipation has been called *synaxis, communio,* communion, which means not only communion with God, but also mutual community among men; a community which is misunderstood and misused if it is not conceived and realized as an alliance from which nobody must be excluded by any arbitrary restriction. A better and deeper foundation of human solidarity cannot, I think, be conceived of, but it is also true that wherever the true solidarity of men is realized or even longed for, this universal meal-community, knowingly or not, is in preparation, no matter how the key words go: democracy, realm of freedom, classless society; provided (this is very important), provided that one's own dictatorship, and the discrimination against or even the liquidation of the others are not on the program at the same time; for in this case everything is depraved from the beginning.

The relation to our topic "hope" is closer than it might seem, for wherever people imagine and strive for the realization of fraternity among men as the essence of what we are hoping for, there is *eo ipso* an underground connection to the elementary hope of Christendom.

The great Christian theology has always said, whoever as a non-Christian is convinced that God, in a way which is pleasing to Him, will be the deliverer of man, believes in the way of implicit faith in Christ. We should also, I think, speak of an implicit corresponding hope.

Thus, whoever summons all his energy of hope for the dream of a perfect human community wherein man is "man" to his neighbour and no longer "wolf" (as Ernst Bloch puts it), and the goods of life are justly distributed, he is participating in the hope of Christendom. And the implicitly faithful non-Christian, who often enough outrivals the declared Christian by his living and serious faith, may likewise overtop him by the ardour of his hope, whose religious absoluteness, perhaps in opposition to the heralded program, seems to show how much the expectation in fact aims at something that cannot be brought about by any human activity for changing the world.

On the other hand, such correspondences can only be perceived from the side of explicit faith and hope. To put it more aggressively: if the Christians do not perceive these underground conformities and call them by their proper names, nobody in the world will perceive them, which means that they will remain mute and without any historical effect. Everybody knows how much remains to be done in this field.

But correspondences and conformities do not yet mean identity, and the distinguishing of Christianity is also an everlasting task. In conclusion I should make a short remark on one of the points of difference, namely on the non-fixability of the object of hope (of 'the' hope).

Gabriel Marcel several times formulates the profound insight that 'the' hope always reaches beyond the objects through which it had originally been kindled, and that 'the' hope loses the best of it as soon as man makes conditions and even as soon as he tries to imagine concretely what he is hoping for.

True hope keeps itself open for a fulfilment which surmounts every conceivable human plan. Whoever is stamped by this true hope will direct the energy of his heart not so much towards the militant carrying-through of defined plans or eschatological visions of order (whereby, as everybody knows, the solidarity of mankind has been trampled down often enough), but on the contrary, he will direct the energy of his heart towards the daily realization of what is 'now' good and just. I surmise that this may be the truest and the most human form of historical activity. This surmise has nothing to do with any reluctance to face the radicalism of great political decisions, and even less with any lack of confidence in the future of human history, but it does have to do with the mistrust of any limitation and fixation of the object of our hope.

The reason for this mistrust has been formulated very adequately by the German poet Konrad Weiss, adequately insofar as he avoids every all-too-positive phrase. He says: "Every attempt to outline a fixed image of the future of mankind is burdened with the heavy paradox that it is not humanity or mankind which is the goal of the Incarnation."

On the Unavoidable Dilemma of a Non-Christian Philosophy

It is, as everybody knows, quite common to discuss the problematic character of Christian philosophy, if not its impossibility. This time, on the contrary, my concern is to pose a question which has been discussed very rarely; it is the question of how an intendedly non-Christian philosophy is possible. Is there not an inherent dilemma in the very idea of a non-Christian philosophy?

Perhaps I should make here some preliminary remarks in order to clarify the meaning of this question. First of all, by a non-Christian philosophy I do not mean, let us say, the philosophy of Hinduism or of China (insofar as these are not yet decisively influenced by Western ideas). My thesis is concerned exclusively with the sphere of Western civilization and the kind of philosophy which has been dominant in the Western world during the last two or three centuries, meaning the philosophy of rationalism. Moreover, 'philosophy' is taken here in the sense which the great founders of occidental philosophy (Pythagoras, Plato, Aristotle) had in mind whenever they used this term. Although it is impossible to expound in short all the ramifications of this old concept of philosophy, two of its most important elements must be mentioned.

First, we should not consider the literal meaning of the Greek word 'philo-sophia' to be something merely incidental. The saying of Pythagoras that no man can be called wise, 'sophos,' but at most a loving seeker of wisdom, 'philo-sophos,' has been interpreted rather seriously by Plato as a matter of principle. For Plato, philosophizing is nothing but the aiming at a wisdom which God alone really possesses. Not even Solon and Homer, he says, have this wisdom; and, on the other hand, none of the gods philosophizes. Yet not only Plato, who may be somewhat suspect as a "religious thinker," but also Aristotle, the founder of a more sober and critical philosophy, says more or less the same thing. According to him, not only is the question of what is real (*Ai Ao on?*) a question which has always been asked and is asked today and will be asked forever; he even maintains that this question, at bottom, tends to an answer which can be known only by God. And this is the reason why Aristotle gives philosophy in the primary sense, i.e. metaphysics, the name 'theology.' Thus, this first element of the original concept of philosophy means (at least) its systematic, unprejudiced openness to theology.

The second element is this: to pose and to ponder a truly philosophical question (for instance, what is cognition? or, what is spirit? or, what does really happen whenever a human being dies?) means always at the same time to inquire after the structure of reality and existence as a whole. Whoever asks a really philosophical question is *eo ipso* compelled to speak of "God and the world." It is this which distinguishes philosophy from science. The medical scientist who investigates the cause

Dilemma of a Non-Christian Philosophy

of a specific infectious disease is not concerned with the world as a whole; he is not even *allowed* to speak of "God and the world," whereas the man who probes the ultimate meaning of sickness in its totality certainly would not do justice to his subject if he refused to think of human existence as a whole, if he refused to start (so to speak) from Adam and Eve. In fact this is exactly what happens in Plato's *Symposium*. The question of the meaning of Eros is first answered by sociology, psychology, biology; but then Aristophanes comes along and says: You cannot expect to know anything adequate about the ultimate meaning of Eros unless you consider what happened to human nature in the beginning of man's history, whereupon he tells the myth of man's original completeness and perfection, of his fall into sin, and of its punishment. He starts, in other words, from Adam and Eve. Or, in the Platonic dialogue *Menon*, when the rational discussion on the nature of teaching and learning has come to a dead end, Socrates says, "Now it becomes necessary to turn to those who are wise in the divine affairs." And who are those who are wise in divine affairs, and where to find them? Socrates (and Plato, too) do not hesitate for a moment to give an answer to this question. Their answer refers to the super-rational sphere of myth, inspiration, revelation, theology. And again even Aristotle does not refuse an answer of this kind. It is one of the most exciting results of Werner Jaeger's classic book on Aristotle: Also behind the far more abstract Ontology of the Aristotelian Metaphysics is to be found the *credo ut intelligam*. Nowadays, if we were to put that same question to an educated orthodox Hindu, we would receive a quite similar answer. But a secularized modern European or North American would know neither what "wisdom in divine affairs" could possibly mean nor where it could be found.

This is the point at which the topic of this short meditation comes into sight: the dilemma of a philosophy which does not acknowledge or even know either myth or theology, but nevertheless still claims to be what Pythagoras, Plato and Aristotle called 'philosophy.' From the Platonic-Aristotelian point of view, the idea of Christian philosophy does not need any defence or justification. But it is exceedingly difficult if not impossible to find an answer to the question, how there can be, in our Western world, such a thing as an explicitly non-Christian philosophy (granted, I repeat, that by philosophy one does not understand anything different from what was meant by this word when it was coined for the first time). In Western civilization there are clearly no analogies to the myths, the "wisdom in divine affairs," the teachings of the cultic mysteries, the sacred tradition handed down by the Ancients who, as Plato says, were the first receivers of a divine message; all this has disappeared out of the modern world-view—unless we assume that it has been absorbed and preserved (and, of course, also purified and unexpectedly perfected) in Christian revelation, faith and theology. If this assumption is true, are we not confronted then by the crucial alternative, either to deny that many-voiced super-rational counterpoint of world-interpretation and consequently to give up what was traditionally called philosophy, or to preserve that essential counterpoint by being systematically open to Christian theology?

At this point I am prepared to meet the counter-question: is it not absurd to maintain that in our Western world there should exist no non-Christian philosophy which deserves the name of philosophy? To this question I give a two-fold answer.

First, there are several forms of modern 'philosophy' which expressly do not intend or claim to be philosophy in the old sense at all, but instead are just special sciences, understandable and of interest only to experts. I am thinking of 'linquistic analysis' and the so-called 'scientific philosophy' in general.

The second part of my answer is more complicated. A non-Christian philosophy, in which every element of the Christian tradition has been completely eliminated, is a very rare phenomenon in our Western world. When for instance Descartes answers the question of why a clear and distinct perception must necessarily be true by referring to the veracity of God, who cannot possibly deceive us, then he clearly relies on that same tradition of faith which he claims to exclude on principle. Or when Immanuel Kant in his essay on religion quotes the Bible some seventy-five times, he quite apparently does not remain, as the title of his essay says, "within the limits of mere reason." Of course, we cannot on this account speak of a piece of Christian philosophy, but can it be called altogether and totally non-Christian? Consider that Jean Paul Sartre, whose existentialism claims to be the most radical form of non-Christian philosophy, could not even be understood by a pagan nihilist of antiquity, let us say, by the sophist Gorgias. "There is no human nature, because there is no God who could have conceived and designed it." One has to be a Christian in order to be able to understand this sentence!

It has been said (incidentally in a very serious critical report on one of my earlier books in a Philosophical Review): "Philosophy is at present under a double threat: of being drained of all humanistic value by reduction to semantics and logic or of being swallowed by obscure, ambiguous and inadequate theology. The left liberals in philosophic thought need to meet this challenge by formulating a philosophy that avoids both dangers." The first sentence has my full agreement, especially since it seems to imply that not every theology must necessarily be "obscure, ambiguous and inadequate." But whether the "left liberals in philosophic thought," they above all, will be able and willing to accept a non-obscure, non-ambiguous and adequate theology, this is something I venture to doubt very much. And it is precisely in this improbability that the dilemma of a non-Christian philosophy unavoidably consists.

On Leisure

Whoever speaks of leisure today is already defending himself; he is on the defensive, he is offering resistance against what seems, at first sight at least, a stronger adversary. Matters are made no easier by the fact that instead of being someone else, this adversary is within ourselves. We are involved in an inner controversy and dispute. Worse still, if questioned, the defender is unable to state with any great precision exactly what he is defending. If, for instance, we accept the Aristotelian statement that "we work in order to have leisure," we are forced to admit that we do not know exactly what it implies. This, I think, is simply the factual situation from which we have to start.

The first question we must ask ourselves is: What is leisure? What is the meaning of the conception in the great humanist European tradition? A useful way of seeking an answer to this question seems to be to begin by considering the opposing force; that is to say, the overestimation of the value of work. But there again is a difficulty, because 'work' may mean various things–at least three things, in fact. In the first place, it may merely mean 'activity' in general. But somebody else could possibly come along and say: I would speak of 'work' only if there is more than mere activity; namely, if there is toil, trouble, labor, effort. And still another could say: I speak of 'work' only if there is a useful activity—useful in the social sense of the word; it has to be a contribution to the common need, a social function.

To which of these three meanings do we refer when we speak of overestimating the value of work? My answer would be: "To all three!" For we do place too high a value on activity in general, as well as on all effort and difficulty, and, last but not least, on man's function in society. This, in fact, is the three-headed Gorgon for any would-be defender of leisure.

What then is wrong? I would say first that what is wrong is the incapacity of accepting and receiving, the hardening of the heart that refuses to be passive in any sense, an inability to let things happen. It is that unconditional activity about which Goethe once remarked that "it necessarily ends in bankruptcy." And I think this kind of bankruptcy is not beyond the realm of our contemporary experience.

Every false idea has, so to speak, its 'insanity form,' a formulation in which its absurdity openly appears. Here is the insanity and madness form of that overestimation of activity: "Every action has some meaning, even crime; to be passive, on the contrary, is always senseless"—a statement to be found in the *Conversations with Hitler* reported by Hermann Rauschning. This, of course, is pure folly and perfectly absurd. But 'milder' forms of this brand of insanity are, I believe, quite universally characteristic of the modern world. And if we look at the 'worker,' that is, at modern man in so far as he is already characterized by that overestimation of activity, then we really can see how much his face is marked by the distinguishing features of tension and exertion, distinguishing it from the typical face of, let us say, his grandparents.

Overestimation of the value of effort and difficulty is, strange as it may seem, a real phenomenon too. It may even be said that the average ethical standards of the 'respectable' modern individual are based largely on an exaggerated respect for difficulty. Where there is no difficulty, there seems to be no true morality. The very concept of moral law seems to be contrary to man's natural bent, thus: the more difficult a thing, the higher it is in the order of goodness. The German poet Friedrich Schiller aimed a shaft of irony at this attitude in his witty verse:

> *How gladly would I help my friends,*
> *but, alas, it is a pleasure.*
> *Thus it vexes me often, that I can*
> *claim no virtue therein.*

The 'ancients'–the Greek philosophers Plato and Aristotle, as well as the teachers of Western Christendom–did not believe that the good is difficult by its very nature, and hence difficult in all circumstances. They were well aware that the highest manifestations of human morality are even effortless, always and necessarily, since by their very essence they spring from love. Nor can the highest forms of knowledge, such as the lightning flash of genius or religious contemplation, be considered 'mental effort,' for they too are really effortless and come to us essentially as gifts.

The word 'gift' may indeed be the key to the problem. Anyone who considers the strange preference for everything that is difficult, which has made the distinguishing mark of modern man his readiness to suffer pain (a much more typical trait, I believe, than his much-condemned 'pleasure-seeking'), must pause to wonder whether the origin of this attitude does not lie in the refusal to accept a gift of any kind, no matter what its source. The Christian idea of man, on the other hand, is based on the conception that in the beginning there is always a gift.

One of the outstanding characteristics of modern society is its overemphasis on social function and utility. Here we are entering a discussion which clearly is more than just theoretical. When we consider the totalitarian 'five-year plans,' we see that their worst feature is not so much the fact of planning but rather their claim to constitute the only yardstick by which to index the whole of human activities, including, for example, university life and the individual use of spare time. We should not, however, forget that in a politically non-totalitarian world, the dictatorship of sheer utility can still be effective.

It may be useful to recall an old and, as it may seem at first sight, old-fashioned distinction—the distinction between *artes liberales* and *artes serviles*; that is to say, between free and servile activities. This distinction means that there are forms of human activity which are meaningful in themselves and which do not aim at an end beyond themselves, and there are, on the other hand, human activities which do aim at an end beyond themselves, which serve other purposes whose value lies in something more than just their utility. Thus when I put the question of the rights of the free activities and of the liberal arts, and when I translate that question into the jargon of the totalitarian world of labour, then it suddenly comes to light how topical and acute a question it is. Such a translation would sound like this: Is there any sphere of human activity, one might even say of human life, that cannot be or does not need to be justified in terms of a 'five-year plan'?

It goes without saying that the answer given by man, in so far as he is already stamped by the overvaluation of social function and utility, will be: No! There must not be such a thing as free, non-useful activity; man is a functional being; free activity which serves no social purpose is undesirable and must be eliminated; man is a 'worker' and nothing else. Once again, the view held by the ancients is diametrically opposite. They say that the non-useful, too, has its rights in human affairs and that a full human existence cannot be contained within an exclusively workaday life; that, on the contrary, the fulfilment of human life lies beyond the limits of useful work.

If we think back to the idea of leisure from the viewpoint of that threefold overestimation of the value of labour and work, it will immediately be clear that there is no room for this concept in a world limited to 'workers.' Leisure must appear as something wholly strange, without rhyme or reason, as something even morally suspect and inexcusable, as just another word for laziness, idleness, and sloth. And indeed, the two attitudes are quite irreconcilable, the idea of leisure being utterly opposed to the concept of the 'worker' in all three aspects of which we have spoken.

Leisure opposes the overestimation of activity. Leisure, in fact, implies an attitude of non-activity, of inward calm, of silence; it means not being busy but letting things happen. I have said: silence. Leisure is a form of that particular silence which is simply a prerequisite for hearing; only the silent hear. Leisure is a receptive attitude of mind which allows the individual to be absorbed into the reality of the world. I would even dare say: A man at leisure is not unlike a man asleep (but "men asleep, too, are active in the happenings of the world" as Heraclitus said). And perhaps we should not forget that the popular saying that God sends his good gifts in sleep, is in fact a sentence from the Bible. Is it not true that the great and imperishable insights visit a man in his moments of leisure only?

Leisure opposes the overestimation of toil and difficulty. Leisure has to be understood as an attitude of celebration, and celebration means not only something different from toil, but the contrary of it. Leisure is not possible unless man is at one with himself and at one with the world. Now, the meaning of the celebration of a feast has always been the same: the affirmation of man's fundamental accord with God and with himself and with the world. This accord, which does not mean a superficial optimism, is an indispensable presupposition of both leisure and the celebration of a feast. And the incapacity for leisure indeed seems to imply the incapacity for celebrating a feast. We shall have to come back to this point once more.

Leisure opposes excessive emphasis on man's social function. Indeed, leisure implies the release of the individual from his social functions as a 'worker.' And it means something entirely different from, say, a break within the working hours. That break–whether it lasts one hour or three weeks–has as its purpose "recovery from work for the sake of work." It is just a link in the chain of work; it exists only in terms of work. Leisure, on the contrary, has not primarily the purpose that the individual may work continually without collapsing, but rather that, while fulfilling his particular utility functions, he may remain a man–which means capable of seeing the whole of life and the whole of the world, and also of feeling himself as a being who essentially has to do with the whole.

True culture cannot thrive unless its seeds are sown in leisure–if we understand 'culture' to mean something beyond the mere necessities of physical existence. Now the crucial question arises: how might it become possible to maintain and defend and even reconquer the rights and claims of leisure, considering the claims of 'total work' which are invading every sphere of life? For there is no doubt that the world of the 'worker,' the mere 'workaday world,' is taking shape with utterly dynamic and, one is tempted to say, even with demoniac force. What can be done to call a halt to the progress of the dictatorship of labour? If the lifeblood of culture is leisure, what does leisure itself require for its existence? How can we make people capable of enjoying leisure ('acting' leisure, as the Greeks used to say)? How can we save them from becoming mere 'workers,' completely absorbed in the workaday world and its utilities?

I confess that I do not have a simple recipe. What I am perhaps able to do is this: to lead the diagnosis a bit deeper, so that possibly some sort of workable therapy becomes visible. The essential difficulty is that the problem cannot be solved by a simple decision, however well-intentioned. And we can explain why this is so.

Everybody knows that for some time past doctors have been insisting on the importance of leisure for health; and they are undoubtedly right. But it is quite impossible to enjoy leisure in order to remain healthy or to become so. There are certain things which can only be done for their own sake. It is impossible to do them so that something else may occur. For instance, nobody can love a human being 'in order to'....

A genuine order cannot be overturned or perverted. Although it may be true that, as some psychiatrists say, the man who is in the habit of saying his nightly prayers sleeps the better for it, no one could say his prayers with that in mind. Whatever is an end in itself cannot be degraded to a means; it is not only incongruous, it simply does not work. You cannot convert people to leisure by telling them how wholesome and beneficial it is. They will never 'act' leisure, not even in order to save our Occidental culture, unless they experience it to be significant in itself.

Perhaps leisure will be valued for itself if we remember that the soul of leisure is celebration. Celebration is the point at which the three elements of leisure merge together: first, non-activity and rest; second, ease and the absence of toil and effort; third, release from workaday tasks and functions. Thus, leisure can only be made possible on the same basis as the celebration of a feast. That basis is, put briefly, that man feels at one with the world and with himself; that he gives his assent to reality at large.

It has been made clear already that this has nothing to do with superficial optimism, but if you do not feel that the world is basically 'good' and that everything is 'in order,' you are simply unable to celebrate a feast no matter how much spare time and money you have.

If this is true, another unavoidable truth follows: The highest known expression of the feeling of being at one with the world as a whole is the praise of God, the worship of the Creator. Having said this, we have defined the true basis of leisure, since the celebration of a feast and leisure derive from the same source. Leisure cannot come about and remain alive unless it is fed by the springs of divine worship. Cut off from that origin, leisure becomes idleness, and work inhuman, which explains the alternatives facing the modern world: inhuman work on the one side and, on the other side, the mere killing of time and boredom.

I believe that we must, however, be prepared to face the fact that many people find this truth rather disagreeable and will go to enormous lengths to escape its consequences. For instance, they may attempt to institute artificial celebrations which manage, by means of an enormous show and the support of political power, to create the false impression of real feasts. In reality, as we know from the French Revolution and the totalitarian regimes of our time, the 'organized recreation' of such pseudo-celebrations is nothing but an even more agitated form of work.

It would be a mistake to think that the theory of the religious basis of leisure and culture is specifically a Christian one. Perhaps what we usually speak of as 'secularism' is not so much a refusal of Christianity as the loss of certain fundamental beliefs and attitudes, which form part of man's natural store of wisdom. The theory of leisure and worship seems to me to belong to this heritage.

Before the Christian era, in fact, it was embodied in an image drawn from mythology by Plato, who asked whether man, so clearly destined for toil and effort, should be allowed at any time to pause for rest. The answer was that such relief from man's labours really exists: "The gods, taking pity on mankind, born to work, laid down the succession of recurring Feasts to restore them from their fatigue and gave them the Muses, and Apollo their leader, and Dionysos, as companions in their Feasts, so that nourishing themselves in festive companionship with the gods, they should stand upright again."

These last words remind me of an old Russian saying–of course, a pre-Bolshevistic one: "Work does not make one rich, but round-shouldered." Below the surface meaning of this saying seems to lie the idea that man, not only outwardly but also inwardly, can become servile and that he can possibly imprison himself in the enclosed realm of total work. Plato says, only in celebrating divine worship does man lose that shape of a slave.

Aristotle expressed the same thought in his more straightforward way. He declared that man cannot live a life of leisure in so far as he is man, but only in so far as something divine dwells within him.

INDEX

Aquinas, Thomas 14, 45
Adam 26, 53
American Federation of
    Labour 17
Apollo 66
Aristotle 51-52, 54, 59, 66
Aristophanes 53
Augustine, St. 1

Balthasar, Hans Ursvon 47
Baudelaire 43-44
Bloch, Ernst 40, 49
Brecht, Bertolt 21, 36
Briand, Aristide 19

Caillois, Roger 20
Cain 26
Chesterton, G.K. 7
Chrysostom 8
Comte, Auguste 9

David, Jacques Louis 15
de Chardin, Pierre Teilhard
    21, 35, 37, 42, 45
de Scudéry, Mademoiselle 19
Descartes 55
Dionysos 66
Diotima 30
Dostoevski 44

Eisner, Kurt 2, 22
Engels, Friedrich 29, 47
Eve 53

Galileo 36
Goethe 58
Gorki, Maxim 19
Gorgias 55
Gorgon 58

Heraclitus 62
Hitler 58
Homer 52
Huxley, Julian 8

Jaeger, Werner 53
Jaspers, Karl 26
Jungmann, Josef Andreas 9

Kant, Immanuel 25-26, 42
Kerény, Karl 5
Kierkegaard, Soren 10, 26
King of England 38
King of Poland 38
Koprowski, Hilary 39

Lec Stanislaus 44
Lorenz, Konrad 26

Marcel, Gabriel 29, 40, 50

Newman, John Henry 42
Nietzsche, Friedrich 1, 7, 10,
    21, 43

Plato 30, 47-48, 51-54, 59, 66
Plügge, Herbert 31-32
Pythagoras 51-52, 54

Queen of Sweden 38

Rahner, Karl 41, 45
Rauschning, Hermann 44, 58
Robespierre 15
Rousseau, Jean Jacques 9

Sarte, Jean Paul 9, 55
Schiller, Friedrich 59
Socrates 53
Solovjev 47
Solon 52

Trotzky, Leon 19

Weiss, Konrad 50

DATE DUE

HIGHSMITH   # 45220